GUINEA PIGS

by Katie Marsico

Children's Press®

An Imprint of Scholastic Inc.
New York Toronto London Auckland Sydney
Mexico City New Delhi Hong Kong
Danbury, Connecticut

Content Consultant
Dr. Stephen S. Ditchkoff
Professor of Wildlife Sciences
Auburn University
Auburn, Alabama

Photographs ©: age fotostock/David Hosking/FLPA: 8, 9; Alamy
Images: 6, 7 (Abby Rex), 4, 5 background, 24, 25 (FLPA); Dreamstime:
1, 46 (Alptraum), 2 background, 3 background, 44 background, 45
background (June M Sobrito), 20, 21 (Patrizio Martorana); Jenna
Casciano: 2, 3, 14, 15; Media Bakery: 16 (Andrey), 34, 35 (Arco
Images/Wegner, Petra"), 39 (Ron Levine); Science Source/Carolyn A.
McKeone: 30, 31; Shutterstock, Inc.: 36, 37 (Agustin Esmoris), 5 bottom,
40 (Vitalinka); Superstock, Inc.: 28, 29 (Animals Animals), 32, 33 (Florian
Kopp/imagebro/imagebroker.net), 18, 19 (imagebroker.net), cover, 12,
13 (Juniors); The Image Works/Tollkühn/ullstein bild: 26, 27; Thinkstock:
22, 23 (Lari Huttunen), 5 top, 10, 11 (Michael Blann).

Map by Bob Italiano

Library of Congress Cataloging-in-Publication Data
Marsico, Katie, 1980– author.
  Guinea pigs / by Katie Marsico.
    pages cm. — (Nature's children)
  Audience: Ages 9–12.
  Audience: Grades 4 to 6.
  Includes bibliographical references and index.
  ISBN 978-0-531-20663-8 (lib. bdg.) — ISBN 978-0-531-21656-9
(pbk.)
  1. Guinea pigs—Juvenile literature. I. Title. II. Series: Nature's children
(New York, N.Y.)
  QL737.R634M37 2014
  599.35'92—dc23   2014001510

Printed in China 62
SCHOLASTIC, CHILDREN'S PRESS, and associated logos are
trademarks and/or registered trademarks of Scholastic Inc.

1 2 3 4 5 6 7 8 9 10 R 24 23 22 21 20 19 18 17 16 15

Guinea Pigs

Class	Mammalia
Order, Suborder	Rodentia, Hystricomorpha
Family, Subfamily	Caviidae, Caviinae
Genus	Cavia
Species	Cavia porcellus
World distribution	Worldwide
Habitats	Indoor cages
Distinctive physical characteristics	Four feet with claws; hair can be short, long, smooth, coarse; colored with various shades of brown, red, tan, and white; small eyes; blunt nose; stubby ears; 6 to 10 inches (15 to 25 centimeters) long; weighs 2 to 3 pounds (0.9 to 1.4 kilograms); males are typically larger than females; stocky body with stubby legs and no tail
Habits	Able to reproduce at three to six weeks old; social animal that lives in groups shaped by competition for dominance; can achieve short bursts of speed; grazes frequently; lives four to eight years if properly cared for; rubs against people, animals, and objects to leave a scent indicating ownership; can reproduce up to five times a year
Diet	Juveniles and adults eat a blend of store-bought pellets, mixed grasses and hay, and fresh fruits and vegetables; newborn pups drink milk from their mothers

Contents

CHAPTER 1

Popcorn, Pigs, or Rodents?

At first, the guinea pig at the pet store seems like it might be asleep. It sits quietly in the bedding, only occasionally moving to twitch its nose or scratch an itch. Then, as if startled by a firecracker, the animal jumps straight up in the air. Its motion almost resembles popcorn popping!

Within seconds, another guinea pig emerges from a plastic tube. Suddenly, strange noises echo throughout the store. The air is filled with a series of chirps, whines, hisses, and chatters. Every once in a while, the guinea pigs sniff each other or touch noses. The cage comes alive as they communicate.

Guinea pigs aren't actually pigs at all. They're stocky, tailless rodents. Because their species name is *Cavia porcellus*, guinea pigs are sometimes referred to as cavies. While they have several wild relatives, guinea pigs do not exist naturally in the wilderness. Instead, people often keep them as domestic pets.

Guinea pigs like hiding in tubes such as the one shown here.

Providing a Proper Home

As pets, guinea pigs require a proper environment to remain healthy. Depending on how many cavies are living there, a cage should measure anywhere from 7.5 to 13 square feet (0.7 to 1.2 square meters). It is important that guinea pigs have enough room to exercise. Veterinarians recommend lining the floors of guinea pig homes with 2 to 3 inches (5 to 7.6 centimeters) of torn paper. Guinea pigs do best in room temperatures ranging from 65 to 75 degrees Fahrenheit (18 to 24 degrees Celsius).

Guinea pig owners can add a variety of objects to the cage to keep their pets happy. Toys and chew treats help give guinea pigs something to do when people aren't around to play. Plastic tubes provide them with places to hide if they do not want to be around people.

Guinea pigs like to come out of their cages and play with their owners.

Colorful Creatures

No two guinea pigs look exactly alike. Their hair can be short or long. Some are even completely hairless! Sometimes a cavy's fur is smooth, but it can also be coarse. These rodents are various shades of brown, red, tan, and white. They can have solid coloring or patterns of splotches and spots.

In addition to having stocky bodies, guinea pigs have stubby legs and ears. Both their front and hind feet feature claws. They also have small eyes, blunt noses, and whiskers on their faces.

Adult guinea pigs measure 6 to 10 inches (15 to 25 cm) long. They typically weigh 2 to 3 pounds (0.9 to 1.4 kilograms). In general, male cavies tend to be slightly larger than females. Babies, or pups, are 3 to 4 inches (7.6 to 10 cm) long at birth. Their weight ranges from 2.5 to 3.5 ounces (71 to 99 grams).

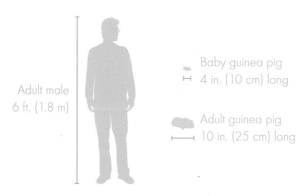

Adult male
6 ft. (1.8 m)

Baby guinea pig
4 in. (10 cm) long

Adult guinea pig
10 in. (25 cm) long

Guinea pigs sometimes have multicolored fur.

CHAPTER 2

Common Characteristics

Guinea pigs were specially bred to be domestic animals. Pet guinea pigs rarely face threats from predators. However, they still have some of the traits and skills that their ancestors used to survive in the wild. For example, guinea pigs are famous for having a "flight-over-fight" reaction when threatened. This means that they would rather flee than try to scare away or overpower the threat. Most veterinarians recommend that cavies be kept indoors. If taken outdoors, they face a number of wild predators. These include snakes, hawks, foxes, and raccoons.

Pet owners have to practice caution with their guinea pigs even when the animals are kept indoors. Other pets, such as dogs and cats, often pose a risk to cavies. Owners can help reduce these dangers by housing guinea pigs in a sturdy cage with a lock.

Under close supervision, other pets can sometimes safely play with guinea pigs.

Speeding Up and Standing Still

Guinea pigs depend a great deal on their human owners. Fortunately, their ability to move fast increases their odds of survival when confronted with a threat. Thousands of years ago, wild guinea pig ancestors traveled across the Andes Mountains. They raced through grass tunnels and along steep slopes. If they had to hide, they were able to squeeze themselves into tiny holes and cracks.

Like their ancestors, guinea pigs can achieve short bursts of speed if they are trying to escape. They aren't good climbers, but they are capable of changing direction quickly. In fact, some people say that cavies don't even appear to pause when they round corners.

In other situations, guinea pigs react to threats by standing completely still. Freezing makes guinea pigs less visible to animals that rely on motion to detect prey. Scientists believe that this behavior also warns other cavies nearby of possible danger.

Because guinea pigs are so speedy, it can be nearly impossible to catch them if they escape outdoors.

Sight and Sound

Cavies are highly alert and depend largely on their eyes and ears to detect changes in their environment. Unlike many other types of rodents, they can see in color. In addition, they have a very broad range of vision. This is because their eyes do not point straight forward. They can see what is happening in front of them and at the same time see what is happening to either side. These traits help make up for the fact that guinea pigs have somewhat poor depth perception. Animals use depth perception to determine how far away something is and to accurately judge the distance between objects.

Guinea pigs have excellent hearing, too. In fact, they tend to be more sensitive to certain sounds than people are. This is especially true when it comes to extremely high-pitched sounds.

FUN FACT! Guinea pigs often sleep with their eyes open!

Guinea pigs tend to be alert and on the lookout for danger.

A Wonderful Nose and Whiskers

Scientists believe that guinea pigs have a highly effective sense of smell. This sense is probably not as developed as a dog's, but it is likely more sensitive than a person's. Cavies rely on their noses to seek out food. They also produce a variety of scents to communicate with each other.

Guinea pigs often rub against objects to leave behind their scent. This scent is a mark of ownership. Sometimes they nuzzle or brush up against other guinea pigs or their human owners for the same reason. The scent left behind serves as a message to other cavies that smell it.

Guinea pigs' whiskers help them learn information about their surroundings. A guinea pig's muzzle is lined with six rows of these sensory hairs. Cavies frequently use their whiskers to figure out how big holes and other openings are. They also depend on them to find their way around dark or unfamiliar spaces.

Guinea pigs bond by nuzzling and rubbing against each other.

Taste Buds and Teeth

Guinea pigs have roughly 17,000 taste buds. This is 8,000 more than human beings have. As a result, guinea pigs can taste a wide variety of foods. Cavies are herbivores. In other words, they eat only plant matter. Veterinarians recommend that owners feed guinea pigs a mixture of store-bought pellets and mixed grasses and hay. Fresh fruit and vegetables are also important parts of a cavy's diet.

It is not uncommon for guinea pigs to eat their own droppings. While this may seem unappetizing, cavies have a good reason for doing it. It is an opportunity to make use of **nutrients** and vitamins that were not absorbed the first time they passed through the rodent's body.

Guinea pigs have 20 **incisors** and **molars** that are constantly growing. This is especially important because the plant matter guinea pigs eat wears down their teeth. Cavies use their incisors to grasp and tear food. They depend on their molars to grind up the food.

Because fruit is high in sugar, guinea pigs should eat it only a few times each week. This makes it a very special treat!

A Mighty Metabolism

Guinea pigs have very fast metabolisms. A metabolism is the rate at which an animal uses energy from food. Animals that have the instinct to flee from threats usually require more energy. This is part of the reason that cavies are always eating. They need a constant supply of food to fuel their metabolism.

A speedy metabolism also helps guinea pigs manage their body temperature. Like all **mammals**, they are warm-blooded. Their body temperature doesn't change simply because the temperature of their environment changes. Normally, cavies have a body temperature of 99°F to 103°F (37°C to 39°C). To stay at this temperature, they must be able to produce body heat in colder weather. Fast metabolisms produce more heat than slow ones. As a result, they allow guinea pigs to keep their temperature where it should be.

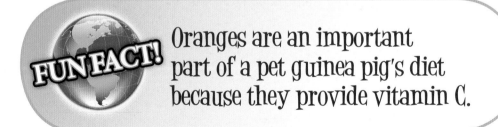

FUN FACT! Oranges are an important part of a pet guinea pig's diet because they provide vitamin C.

Hand-feeding a pet guinea pig both supports its metabolism and makes it more comfortable around people.

CHAPTER 3

A Look at a Cavy's Life

Guinea pigs are social animals. They would rather be with other cavies than on their own. A group of guinea pigs is called a herd. Belonging to a herd helped cavy ancestors survive in the wild. Herds offered added protection against predators. They were also a source of extra warmth in colder environments.

Cavies developed patterns of communication within their herds. Today, they still use their teeth and vocal cords to create a wide variety of sounds. These include chatters, chirps, coos, hisses, purrs, rumbles, shrieks, squeals, whines, and whistles. Each noise has a different meaning. For example, squealing and whistling show excitement. Guinea pigs tend to make a loud "wheeking" sound when they sense they are about to be fed. Meanwhile, a cavy that chatters its teeth is demonstrating a completely different emotion. This sound expresses anger and serves as a warning to stay away.

Some people keep large herds of guinea pigs.

The Meaning of Body Motions

Body language is another form of cavy communication. Jumping straight in the air, or "popcorning," shows happiness and excitement. Touching noses is a form of greeting. When a guinea pig raises its head and bares its teeth, it is displaying aggression.

Cavies also exhibit these last two behaviors to establish their rank within the herd. They may circle and bite one another as well. Females frequently compete with other females for dominance. Males do the same with other males. Dominant animals usually win control over food, water, and preferred areas of a shared home.

In most cases, guinea pigs can be kept together without a problem. The key is making sure each one has enough space. Owners must closely watch their pets—especially male cavies—when they are first introduced. Sometimes less dominant guinea pigs end up suffering from injuries, stress, and even malnutrition.

If your guinea pig jumps into the air when you walk into the room, it is probably happy to see you.

Guinea Pig Reproduction

A guinea pig uses noises and body language to attract a **mate**. Males tend to strut and make a rumbling sound as they prepare to mate with females. Guinea pigs are able to **reproduce** when they are just three to six weeks old. At this point, males are referred to as boars. Females are called sows.

If allowed to mate, guinea pigs will often reproduce up to five times a year. When a sow becomes pregnant, she carries her babies for 59 to 72 days before giving birth. There can be up to eight babies in a guinea pig **litter**. However, the average is usually closer to three.

Unlike most rodents, guinea pigs don't build nests to get ready for the arrival of their young. Babies are typically born at night. Depending on the size of her litter, a sow gives birth to her pups in about 10 to 30 minutes.

Mother guinea pigs are able to care for several babies at once.

Birth and Beyond

Mammals are often born with their eyes closed. They have little to no hair. This is not the case with guinea pigs. Pups look like smaller versions of their parents. Baby cavies enter the world with fur-covered bodies and open eyes. They are alert and almost immediately begin exploring their surroundings.

Like many mammals, guinea pig pups drink their mother's milk. This is not their only source of nutrition, though. Cavies start eating solid foods within a few days of being born. They generally stop nursing after two to three weeks.

Sows feed their pups but usually don't do much else to parent them. Young cavies are fairly independent, even as babies. It doesn't take long for them to figure out how to **groom** themselves and communicate. Most guinea pigs are fully grown by the time they are about 14 months old. With proper care, they live between four and eight years.

Guinea pig pups are ready to run and play shortly after birth.

CHAPTER 4

Past and Present Identity

Guinea pigs belong to a **family** of rodents that first appeared between 26 million and 7 million years ago. Cavies share various characteristics with other members of the Caviidae group. These include three toes on each hind foot and the absence of a tail.

Scientists suspect that early South Americans began domesticating guinea pigs around 5000 BCE. However, they were not bred to be family pets at that time. Instead, cavies were mainly viewed as a food source.

European explorers who visited the Andes Mountains in the 1500s CE brought guinea pigs back home with them. This is roughly the same time that people started keeping them as pets. Today, cavies continue to be raised as **livestock** in certain areas. Guinea pigs are frequently used in scientific research as well. Yet they are perhaps best known as beloved companion animals that have achieved worldwide popularity as pets.

*Farmers in some parts of the world raise
large numbers of guinea pigs for food.*

A Brief Glance at Breeds

There are several different types, or breeds, of guinea pig. Breeds are usually separated by differences in their physical appearance. Not everyone agrees on how many breeds exist, and it's always possible that breeders will develop a new type of cavy. However, the American Cavy Breeders Association (ACBA) currently sets physical standards for 13 varieties.

The texel is one. These guinea pigs have long, soft coats. The texel's body—including its stomach—is covered in tight curls. Because of their hair, texels require regular combing.

The American cavy is another breed listed by the ACBA. American guinea pigs have smooth, short coats. They are one of the most popular types of cavy. So is the teddy, which has kinked hair that seems to stand straight up.

Skinny pigs and Baldwins are famous for having little to no fur. The ACBA doesn't officially recognize skinny pigs or Baldwins. Nevertheless, many breeders sell them to pet owners.

Texel guinea pigs are known for their soft, curly coats.

A Review of Wild Relatives

Cavia porcellus may not be wild, but some of its relatives are. About 15 species of wild cavy exist in the South American wilderness. Scientists believe that domesticated breeds are most closely related to montane, Brazilian, and shiny guinea pigs.

Wild cavies live in **habitats** ranging from mountains and swamps to grasslands, plains, and forests. When not searching for food, they often spend time in **burrows** and small openings in rocks, as well as amid low-lying woody plants called shrubs. In the wilderness, cavies usually belong to herds of 5 to 10 animals. They rely on communication similar to the sounds and body language used by their domestic cousins.

Wild species frequently have long, coarse hair that is some shade of brown or gray. They don't have the wide variety of fur types and colors that pet guinea pigs do. Their hair helps them blend in with their natural surroundings.

Wild cavies are often colored to blend in with their natural surroundings.

CHAPTER 5

Guinea Pigs and People

Humans and guinea pigs share a sometimes complicated relationship. This is partly because people have different ideas about the humane treatment of cavies. Scientists often use them to conduct research. They study how guinea pigs react to everything from medicine to the chemicals in makeup. The purpose is to predict what effects these products will have on humans. Some animal-rights groups think such experimentation is cruel and unnecessary.

Another complicated part of the relationship between humans and guinea pigs is that new pet owners aren't always aware of the care that cavies require. Improper diet and housing lead to unhappy, unhealthy animals. A lack of attention and exercise has the same result. In certain situations, guinea pigs end up neglected or abandoned. This frequently occurs when owners don't understand the responsibilities they take on after purchasing a cavy from the pet store.

People should carefully consider all the responsibilities of pet ownership before getting any animal.

Efforts to Raise Awareness

Fortunately, everyone from veterinarians to animal-welfare groups is working to educate the public about guinea pigs. Their efforts provide an opportunity to learn more about all sides of the issues, such as the role cavies play in scientific research. New owners are being given more information about guinea pigs before bringing one home.

It is important for new owners to understand that cavies can be an eight-year commitment. In addition, people should recognize how quickly guinea pigs reproduce. Allowing them to breed can result in neglected or abandoned pets.

Shelters and rescues attempt to find homes for unwanted cavies. Adoption is frequently less expensive than shopping at a pet store. It is also a chance to help a guinea pig in need.

Cavies and human beings have shared a bond for thousands of years. Today, many people view them as fun, fascinating companions. In exchange for the affection and enjoyment they provide, guinea pigs deserve educated, compassionate caretakers.

With proper care, a guinea pig can be a loving companion and fun playmate for many years.

Words to Know

aggression (uh-GRESH-uhn) — violent or threatening behavior

ancestors (AN-ses-turz) — ancient animal species that are related to modern species

burrows (BUR-ohz) — tunnels or holes in the ground made or used as a home by an animal

domestic (duh-MES-tik) — tamed; people use domestic animals as a source of food or as work animals, or keep them as pets

dominance (DAH-muh-nins) — the state of holding power or influence over others

environment (en-VYE-ruhn-muhnt) — the natural surroundings of living things, including the air, land, and sea

family (FAM-uh-lee) — a group of living things that are related to each other

groom (GROOM) — to take care of one's appearance

habitats (HAB-uh-tats) — the places where an animal or a plant is usually found

humane (hyoo-MAYN) — kind to people or animals

incisors (in-SYE-zurz) — teeth in the front of the mouth that are used for cutting

litter (LIT-ur) — a number of baby animals that are born at the same time to the same mother

livestock (LIVE-stahk) — animals that are kept or raised on a farm or ranch

malnutrition (mal-noo-TRISH-uhn) — sickness or weakness caused by not eating enough food or by eating unhealthy food

mammals (MAM-uhlz) — warm-blooded animals that have hair or fur and usually give birth to live babies; female mammals produce milk to feed their young

mate (MAYT) — an animal that joins with another animal to reproduce

molars (MOH-lurz) — the wide, flat teeth at the back of the mouth used for crushing and chewing food

muzzle (MUHZ-uhl) — an animal's nose and mouth

nutrients (NOO-tree-uhnts) — substances such as proteins, minerals, or vitamins needed by people, plants, and animals to stay strong and healthy

predators (PRED-uh-turz) — animals that live by hunting other animals for food

prey (PRAY) — an animal that's hunted by another animal for food

reproduce (ree-pruh-DOOS) — to produce offspring

rodents (ROH-duhnts) — mammals with large, sharp front teeth that are constantly growing and used for gnawing things

species (SPEE-sheez) — one of the groups into which animals and plants of the same genus are divided; members of the same species can mate and have offspring

Habitat Map

NORTH AMERICA

SOUTH AMERICA

PACIFIC OCEAN

ATLANTIC

Guinea Pig Range

ARCTIC OCEAN

ASIA

EUROPE

AFRICA

PACIFIC OCEAN

OCEAN

INDIAN OCEAN

OCEAN

AUSTRALIA

Find Out More

Books

Beck, Angela. *Guinea Pigs: Keeping and Caring for Your Pet*. Berkeley Heights, NJ: Enslow Publishers, 2014.

Carraway, Rose. *Great Guinea Pigs*. New York: Gareth Stevens Publishing, 2012.

Johnson, Jinny. *Guinea Pigs*. Mankato, MN: A+/Smart Apple Media, 2009.

Visit this Scholastic Web site for more information on guinea pigs:
www.factsfornow.scholastic.com
Enter the keywords **Guinea Pigs**

Index

Page numbers in *italics* indicate a photograph or map.

About the Author

Katie Marsico is the author of more than 100 children's books. She has owned several guinea pigs in her lifetime, and she loves hearing them chitchat and watching them "popcorn" around their cage.